Call of the World

The Incarnational Journey of the Soul

David Spangler

Illustrations by Deva Berg

Other Works by
David Spangler

**To the Power of Incarnation
In Each of Us
To Bless the World**

Acknowledgements

This book is the product of many people's work and creativity. It certainly would not have been possible without the artistic wisdom, skill, and insights of Deva Berg whose pictures grace these pages and bring them to inspiring life. I want to acknowledge all those who have participated in classes and workshops with me over the years in which these images were tested and used and whose comments, insights, and suggestions have been invaluable. You have been my allies in incarnating this material. Thank you very much! And of course, thanks to all my family and to my lovely wife, Julia, who make it all possible for me. And to the unseen, unsung allies and colleagues on the inner worlds who are the true source of this material.

Call ^{of the} World

The Incarnational Journey of the Soul

Illustrations and Cover Art by Deva Berg

Published by Lorian Press
2204 E Grand Ave.
Everett, WA 98201

10 Digit ISBN: 0-936878-40-1
13 Digit ISBN: 978-0-936878-40-9

Spangler/David
Call of the World: *The Incarnational Journey of the Soul*/David
Spangler

First Edition September 2011

Printed in the United States of America

0 9 8 7 6 5 4 3 2 1

www.lorian.org

Contents

Call of the World

The Incarnational
Journey of the Soul

We begin with Light.

The Light that is the heart of all that is.
The Light that is the substance of all that is.
The Light that seeks expression and emerges in infinite
varieties of being.

We are that Light.

The wonder of our lives is that we hold within
    ourselves
The same creative, generative Presence from which
    the universe emerges.

We are each children of Creation,
Children of the Cosmos,
Born of the same substance,
The same Light,
The same Will-to-Be,
The same Will-to-Become.

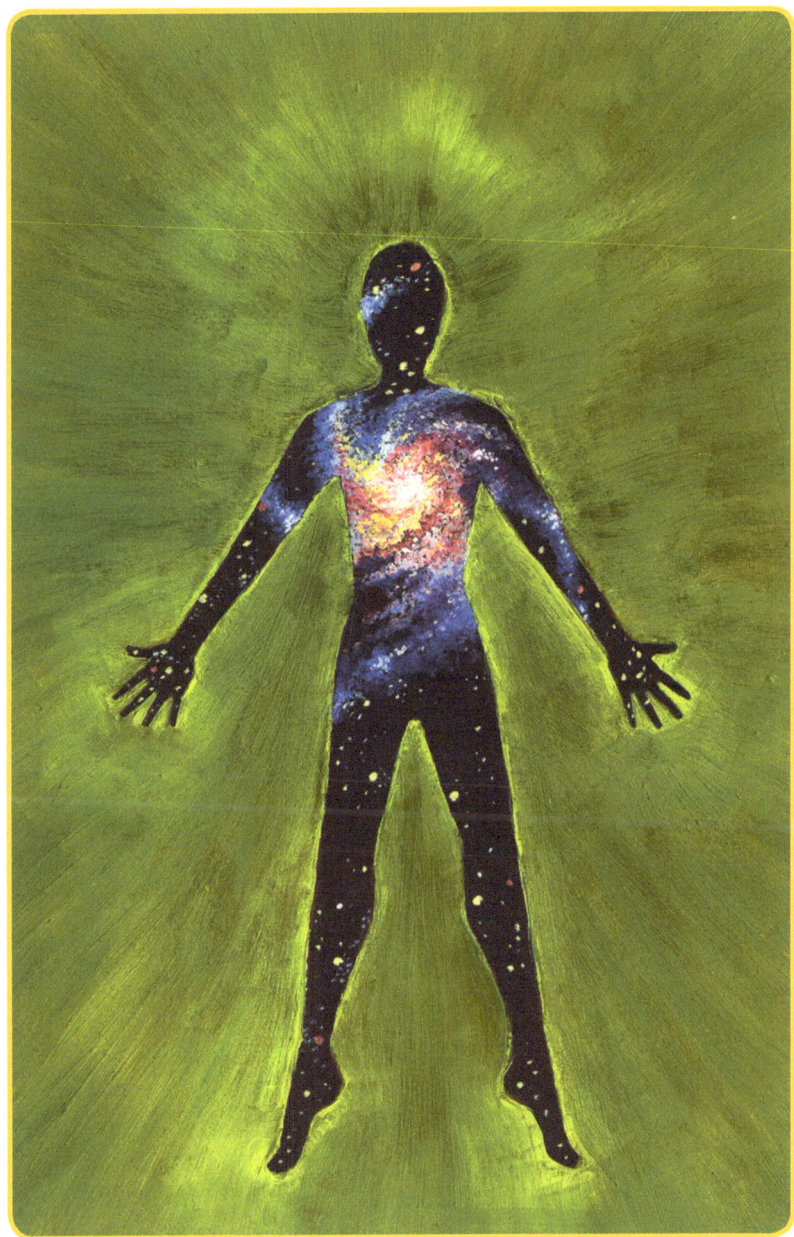

When we come to this world
We step out of a Flow of infinite creative energy, love,
    and Light.
We step into the physical world.
We become creatures of matter,
Partners of the Earth.

Yet, we never lose
Our essential contact with that Flow.
It remains within us,
Part of us,
Always.

The Earth welcomes us.
It has its vision, too:
A vision of all we can become,
A vision of all we can create,
A vision of partnership with Light,
A vision of partnership with Life,
And with the Earth itself.

This vision is a call to each of us,
A call of the world.
We may forget it.
We may remember it.
But it is always there,
Waiting to inspire,
Waiting to inform,
Waiting to be fulfilled.

This vision is part of who we are.

We do not come to Earth aimlessly.
We come in answer to its call,
With intent,
With purpose,
To be a loving partner
To life within this world.

Our intent is a path into the world.
It is a way to connect to the life around us.
It is a way to answer the call.
It does not bar us from the land through which we
        travel.
We can always explore off-road, if we wish.
But it does provide the clearest way
To fulfill who we are
In partnership with the Earth.

When we come to Earth
We join the community of Life.
We see this community about us
In the plants and creatures of the world.
But there are hidden parts as well
Lives that are unseen unless we look
And unless we care to see:
Lives visible and invisible,
Small and Large,
Spirit and Matter.

They are all our kin
In an ecology of being.

We do not walk our path alone.
We have Allies,
Seen and Unseen,
Known and Unknown,
Human
And Other.

When we come to Earth,
We walk the Path of Humanity as well.
We walk in the Path of its Past.
We walk the Path of its Present.
We create the Path to its Future.

When we come to Earth,
We come with Power.
We have the Power to Connect,
To form relationships through which we may co-
    create.

Through a partnership of love and care,
We are wizards,
Shaping the world around us,
Bringing wonders into being,
Helping the Earth reveal its own potentials.

Around ourselves,
We create possibility.
We create a space in which
Opportunities can arise,
Intentions can be held,
And emergence can occur.

We can be architects of potential.

When we come to Earth,
We become Alchemists.

Through our lives, we can transform
Possibility into Reality.
Through our love, we can transform
Hatred into Compassion.
Through our Light, we can transform
Conflict into Wholeness.
Through our caring, we can transform
Fear into Safety.

When we come to Earth,
We have the power to explore.
We have the ability to learn.
We have the capacity to grow.

We can go where no one has gone before.
We can see what no one has seen before.
We can discover what no one has known before.

We need to trust ourselves
And have joy in our courage
To step away from the familiar
Into the Unknown.

Part of the call of the world
Is to know ourselves
And to know the world
In new ways.

When we come to Earth,
We come not as visitors
But to make ourselves a home—
To make ourselves at home.

We come to participate,
To join with others—
Physical and non-physical,
Solid and Spirit—
To build a heaven on Earth,
A place that blesses all of us,
All life, all beings on this world,
And fulfills the vision of wholeness
And Light.
The Call of the World
Planted in our hearts.

We come to be a blessing.

We come that where we pass on our path,
Life unfolds abundantly
And with grace.

We come to discover the Light of our Self
That it may nurture the world.

Most of all
When we come to Earth,
We come to remember
Who we are—
And what is within us.

When we remember this,
We remember the Call of the World.

Call of the World

The Practice of
Incarnational Spirituality

What is Incarnational Spirituality?

Incarnational Spirituality is a new approach to understanding the sacredness of the individual and of his or her relationship to the world.

We usually think of incarnation as simply being in a physical body. After all, the original meaning of the word in Latin was to "make flesh," that is, turning spirit into flesh. We may not think of what processes of spirit have brought this condition about—or may still be active within us in "making us flesh." Nor do we think of what other spiritual resources may be present in us as a result of those processes.

Exploring and understanding the process of incarnation and its effects is what Incarnational Spirituality is about. Basic to this understanding is that incarnation is not simply a condition but is an ongoing process. It is "Life Crafting."

Incarnation is more than just having a body. It is about engagement, wholeness, caring, cooperating. It is about practicing the craft of Life. Incarnational Spirituality offers new perspectives on this craft and practical tools in its expression.

This book, *Call of the World*, is a meditation on the process of incarnation and the spirit that infuses and arises from it. The images are all taken from a card deck, *The Soul's Oracle*, which, along with its manual, gives an in-depth look at this process. This card deck can be used as a study guide, as an aid to meditation, and as an oracle.

In the pages that follow, this book offers four simple practices that can give you some of the flavor of Incarnational Spirituality. If you are interested in knowing more or would like to obtain the card deck itself, *The Soul's Oracle*, there is additional information at the end of this book.

Incarnation is about more than just fulfilling the purposes of your own individual life, important as that may be in the growth of your soul. It is also a collaborative partnership between you, others, the realms of spirit, and the Earth itself in shaping a planet that is a blessing to all. Your incarnation is a response to the Call of the World.

Practice One
Attunement to the Four Principles

Incarnation—whether of a project, a business, or a soul—is a dynamic blend of four elements: Identity, Boundary, Engagement, and Emergence. I call these Principles of incarnation. Although they interact and support each other, we might think of them also as stages, for in many instances they follow one another in a sequence, one leading to the expression of the next. They describe the process of incarnation, the creative loop that goes from inception to fulfillment.

One of the practices of Incarnational Spirituality is to attune to these Principles and understand the unique ways in which they manifest in our lives. More than mere concepts, these Principles are practical tools we can use in a variety of ways, such as when we create projects or seek to manifest something in our lives. Used with insight and skill, they are the keys to building a better world.

IDENTITY

Identity is our intent to respond to the Call of the World.

You come to Earth as an intention made flesh. Knowing the call of the world, your soul responds from a desire to be of service, as well as to learn what Earth has to offer. This desire shapes your unique identity. All incarnation begins with identity, which is intention given form.

The Principle of Identity leads to the others. It initiates. What does this Principle mean to you? How do you experience your own identity? Are you just the content of your autobiography and history, a figment of your own self-reflective imagination, or is there something deeper within you, a presence beyond memory and self-image? How does your identity—your felt sense of who you are—shape your life and the world around you? These are the types of questions that can lead you to a deeper knowledge of who you are, of the Identity from which you emerge, of the intent that is your soul's presence within you.

BOUNDARY

Boundary is how we frame and focus our response to the Call of the World

Boundaries define intent and create the unique space within which an identity can develop and know itself. Boundaries distinguish the "I" from the "not-I," or one "I" from another. Like rivers flowing through and dividing up the land, boundaries allow the One to know itself in myriad and infinite ways.

The Principle of Boundary differentiates. What does this Principle mean to you? How do you experience your boundaries? Where are the edges in your life? How do you create your boundaries? How do you maintain them? What do you let in and include in your life and what to you exclude? How do you go beyond your boundaries if you need to, and what happens when you do? How do your boundaries shape your life and the world around you?

ENGAGEMENT

Engagement is the act of connection and participation that answers the Call of the World

When we engage with the Earth and with others, we form the connections that enable us to participate in the life of the world. Engagement takes us beyond ourselves—beyond our Identity, beyond our boundaries—into collaboration and co-creativity. We become part of shared identities and shared boundaries, with the whole world being the space within which we are at home.

The Principle of Engagement creates relationship. What does this Principle mean to you? How do you experience your connections with others and with the world? What relationships are important to you? How easily do you form connections? How easily do you engage with life and participate in the world? Generally, what is the quality of your engagement? How does your ability to connect and engage shape your life and the world around you?

EMERGENCE

Emergence is what unfolds when we answer the Call of the World

Emergence is the product of engagement and relationship. It is the appearance of that which has been co-created or learned, developed or discovered. It may be unpredicted and novel, taking us by surprise. If incarnation is the planting of the soul in the soil of the Earth, then emergence is the plant and the harvest that results.

The Principle of Emergence creates unfoldment, newness, and the unexpected. What does this Principle mean to you? What do you feel is emerging in your life? How easily do you change and move into new patterns? What are you learning? How are you growing? Is anything new developing in your life? How easily do you deal with change and moving into unknown or new territory and experiences?

Practice Two
The Four Attunements

While there are many ways that Incarnational Spirituality can be practiced, four practices stand out: Attunement to Self, Attunement to Spirit and the Sacred, Attunement to the World, and Blessing. These four practices create a foundation for further incarnational work.

Attunement to Self: This is a practice of self-reflection and self-knowledge. It consists of whatever you may do to gain insights into your character, who you are, and how you express yourself in the world. This is your attunement to the personal side of yourself. It is also a practice of honoring your uniqueness and individuality and the Light within you. Whatever you do to gain greater self-understanding is part of the Attunement to Self.

Attunement to Spirit and the Sacred: This is a practice of looking beyond yourself to the larger world, the larger universe, the larger wholeness of which you are a part. It consists of whatever you may do to understand and align with the spiritual side of the world. This is your attunement to your transpersonal side, to your soul, and to the Sacredness within you that links you in kinship and harmony to everything else in creation.

Attunement to the World: This is a practice of understanding your connection to nature and to the world as a whole. It is also your practice of connection and attunement to others and to humanity as a whole. What does it mean to be a creature upon the earth, part of the biosphere? What does it mean to be part of the human species? What does it mean to contribute to the well-being and wholeness of both? This is your attunement to the larger interconnections and patterns of life and culture of which you are a part. It is the practice of how you engage with the world around you. And if you wish to pursue it, this is also the practice of attunement to the invisible spiritual dimensions of the world.

Blessing: This is a practice of bringing positive spiritual presence and energy into the world around you. It is a practice of compassion and of nourishing life and happiness around you. It is enhancing the goodness and well-being of humanity, the biosphere and the world at large.

Practice Three
The Four Blessings

There are many ways we can bless ourselves, each other and the world around us, but in Incarnational Spirituality, four blessings are particularly important: blessing yourself, blessing the place where you are, blessing whom you are with, and blessing the work or activity you are doing.

Think of the blessings in your life. Think of the blessing that you are or can be to others. Honor yourself as a unique individuation of spiritual Light and sacredness. Bless yourself.

Think of where you are, the place you are currently in. Be aware of all the things around you. Each of them is also a unique manifestation of sacredness. Honor your surroundings and bless them.

Think of the people in your life. If there are others in the place where you are in this moment, think of them as well. These people are also unique manifestations of sacredness, just as you are. Honor them and bless them.

Think of the work that you do in your life. This work or activity is a way you engage with the world and express your incarnational qualities and potentials. How does this work or activity better the world around you? In what way is it a blessing? Honor what you do and bless it.

Practice Four
Your Incarnational Presence

We are four-fold beings.

Part of us arises from the presence of the soul and the transpersonal forces of our essential sacredness.

Part of us arises from nature and the body of the world, from the forces of physics and chemistry, biology and evolution.

Part of us arises from our individual personhood, the forces of psychology acting within our personality.

Part of us arises from our humanity, from the forces of culture and human experience and knowledge.

These four unite in us in an alchemy of incarnation,
creating in each of us a unique presence
that is radiant with Self-Light.

Here is a Practice to attune to this Presence.

Stand facing a direction of your choice.   As you do, attune to your soul, to your transpersonal self, to the Sacred within you. Imagine the felt sense of these forces pouring into your body like wine into a grail. Attune to the felt sense of these forces within your body. Feel yourself as a sacred being.

Turn ninety degrees and face a new direction. As you do, attune to Nature, to the forces of the world, the forces of physics and chemistry, biology and evolution. Feel these forces pouring into your body like wine into a grail. Attune to the felt sense of being a part of nature, a creature of the earth.

Turn ninety degrees and face a new direction. As you do, attune to your everyday personal self, to the forces of experience and life, psychology and learning that shape your sense of who you are. Feel these forces pouring into your body like wine into a grail. Attune to the felt sense of being a unique, individual personality.

Turn ninety degrees and face a new direction. As you do, attune to Humanity and to the forces of culture and history. Feel these forces pour into your body like wine into a grail. Attune to the felt sense of being a human being.

Turn your attention inward to the center of your body and being. Here all these forces come together and combine, and as they do, a unique presence emerges. This Presence is YOU, radiant with Self-Light, drawing all the forces of soul, nature, personality, and humanity together into a wholeness.

Stand in the felt sense of this Presence and feel its Light radiate your body and yourself with blessing. Feel your Self-Light radiating out into the world with blessing.

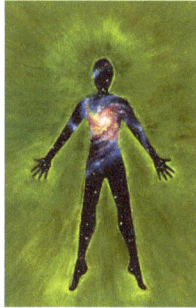

Your Transpersonal Self - Soul and Sacredness

Humanity

Nature
and the World

Your Personal Self

Further Resources

If The Soul's Oracle and the ideas and practice of Incarnational Spirituality interest you, here are some resources you can use to explore them more deeply. Most can be found in the Bookstore on the Lorian website at www.Lorian.org.

Books:

An Introduction to Incarnational Spirituality, by David Spangler; Lorian Press (2011)

Apprenticed to Spirit: The Education of a Soul, by David Spangler; Riverhead Books (2011)

The Gathering Light, by Jeremy Berg; Lorian Press (2010)

Facing the Future, by David Spangler; Lorian Press (2010)

Subtle Worlds: An Explorer's Field Notes, by David Spangler; Lorian Press (2010)

Blessing: The Art and the Practice, by David Spangler; Riverhead Books (2001)

Card Decks:

Manifestation: Creating the life you love, by David Spangler and Deva Berg; Lorian Press (2004)

The Soul's Oracle, by David Spangler and Deva Berg; Lorian Press (2011)

The Card Deck of the Sidhe, by David Spangler and Jeremy Berg; Lorian Press (2011)

Regular Publications:

David's Desk, a free monthly essay on spirituality and current events by David Spangler sent to all on the Lorian mailing list.

Views from the Borderlands, a quarterly journal by David Spangler and others on esoteric and spiritual topics, available by subscription only.

To subscribe to either of these publications, or to receive Lorian's free monthly newsletter, please register at www.lorian.org.

Self-Study Modules (Textbooks, Audio and Video):

Self-study modules on various topics of Incarnational Spirituality plus textbooks that are published transcripts of classes by David Spangler are all available from the Lorian Website.

The Lorian Library:

The Lorian Library is a source of further information. The Lorian Association has offered a Masters of Spiritual Direction degree and a Masters of Contemporary Spirituality. There are a number of theses written by graduate students for their degrees that can be found in the Library on the Lorian Website. The Library has other articles as well. These all throw light on Incarnational Spirituality and its applications as well in a variety of fields.

Classes:

Lorian offers classes and workshops in Incarnational Spirituality and its applications. Please check the Lorian Website to see what is available.

Group Classes:

If you would like to gather and sponsor a group to study some aspect of Incarnational Spirituality, please contact the Lorian office at Info@Lorian.com to see what can be arranged.

Further Work with the Cards:

If you have enjoyed this book and feel you have benefited from the use of these images and practices you may be interested in an expanded version of this material.

The purpose of this book is to introduce some of the practices of Incarnational Spirituality. The images have not been used here in an oracular way. However, it is possible to combine these practices with divination, using various layouts as a basis for oracular work. Complete instructions for this and other layouts as well as expanded descriptions of the incarnational process as described in the cards can be found in *The Soul's Oracle* shown on the following page.

The Soul's Oracle

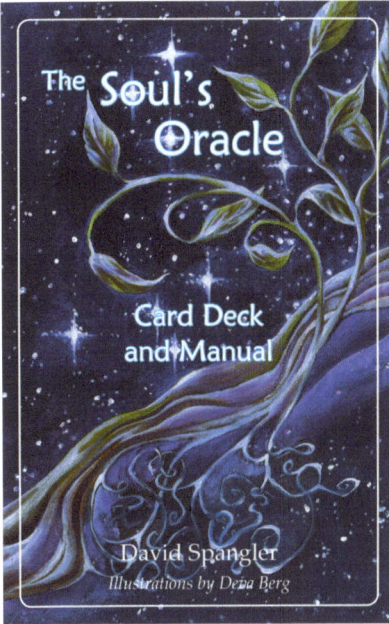

The Soul's Oracle contains an expanded manual describing layouts for divination and the oracular meaning of the cards as well as other material not found in this book. It comes with a premium deck of twenty-seven 3.25 inch X 4.75 inch (Tarot size) cards, a carrying box and pouch for the cards. It also includes seven additional "condition" cards which are used to enhance the oracular uses of this deck but are not part of the meditations in this book.

This card deck and manual can be purchased through the Lorian Association bookstore at www.lorian.org. and through selected bookstores.

www.ingramcontent.com/pod-product-compliance
Lightning Source LLC
Chambersburg PA
CBHW042107110426
42742CB00033BA/19